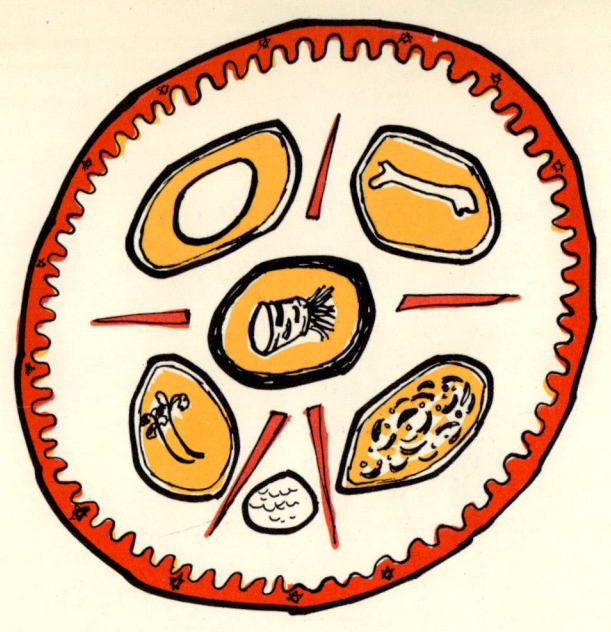

by Hyman and Alice Chanover

with Illustrations by Leonard Kessler

UNITED SYNAGOGUE COMMISSION
ON JEWISH EDUCATION

COPYRIGHT 1956 BY THE UNITED SYNAGOGUE OF AMERICA
Printed in the United States of America.

PESAH IS HERE!

Joel and Mimmy came dashing down the stairs. Their faces were washed and scrubbed. They were all dressed up for the Seder.

"Look at my new bow-tie, Grandma!" cried Joel. "And my new pink dress!" Mimmy pointed, and she twirled round and round on her toes to show it to Grandma.

"My, how nice and grown-up you both look in your new holiday clothes!" Grandma remarked.

"Baby Dan is also wearing something new for Pesaḥ," said Mimmy. "Here he comes down the stairs with Mommy. Doesn't he look cute in his new blue and white suit?"

Somebody else was all dressed up for Pesaḥ, too. Little Pussy. She was jumping down the stairs, bouncety-bounce, one step at a time, wearing a bright yellow ribbon.

"Look, Mimmy," Joel laughed, "even our table is dressed for Yom Tov!"

Indeed it was. The dining room table was wearing a snowy white cloth. In the center stood two shiny candlesticks, tall and straight.

"Hurry, children," called Mommy. "The sun will soon set. It's time to light the Yom Tov candles."

Mommy and Grandma lit the candles. Near them stood the children, *quiet as little mice*.

Baby Dan was so small he couldn't see what was going on. So he stood way up on his little toes and stretched his little neck this way and that to watch the flickering candles.

When Grandma and Mommy finished blessing the candles, they bent down and gave each child a kiss.

"Please, Mommy," pleaded Mimmy, "may we help you set the Seder table?" Mommy smiled and nodded.

So off ran Mimmy to the kitchen to get some forks and spoons and knives. Joel scurried right after her to see what he could bring. Back and forth, back and forth they went. Soon the silverware and the dishes and the wine cups and the napkins and the very special cup for Elijah were set on the table.

Just as Joel was placing the Haggadot on the table—one at each place—the front door opened wide. Daddy and Grandpa were home from the Synagogue.

"Ḥag Same'aḥ, Happy Holiday, everybody," they sang out.
Mimmy and Joel raced to the door to kiss them. Baby Dan tried to run across the carpet as fast as he could. He wanted a kiss, too.

"Is everything ready for the Seder?" Daddy asked.

"Almost," said Mommy. "While you prepare the Seder plate, I can get the three matzot to put into our beautiful matzah cover and Grandpa can fill the wine cups."

Everybody hustled and bustled.

A little while later, Daddy came in from the kitchen holding the big, round Seder plate. "It's all ready," he declared. Mimmy and Joel rushed over to see what the Seder plate looked like. And this is what they saw:

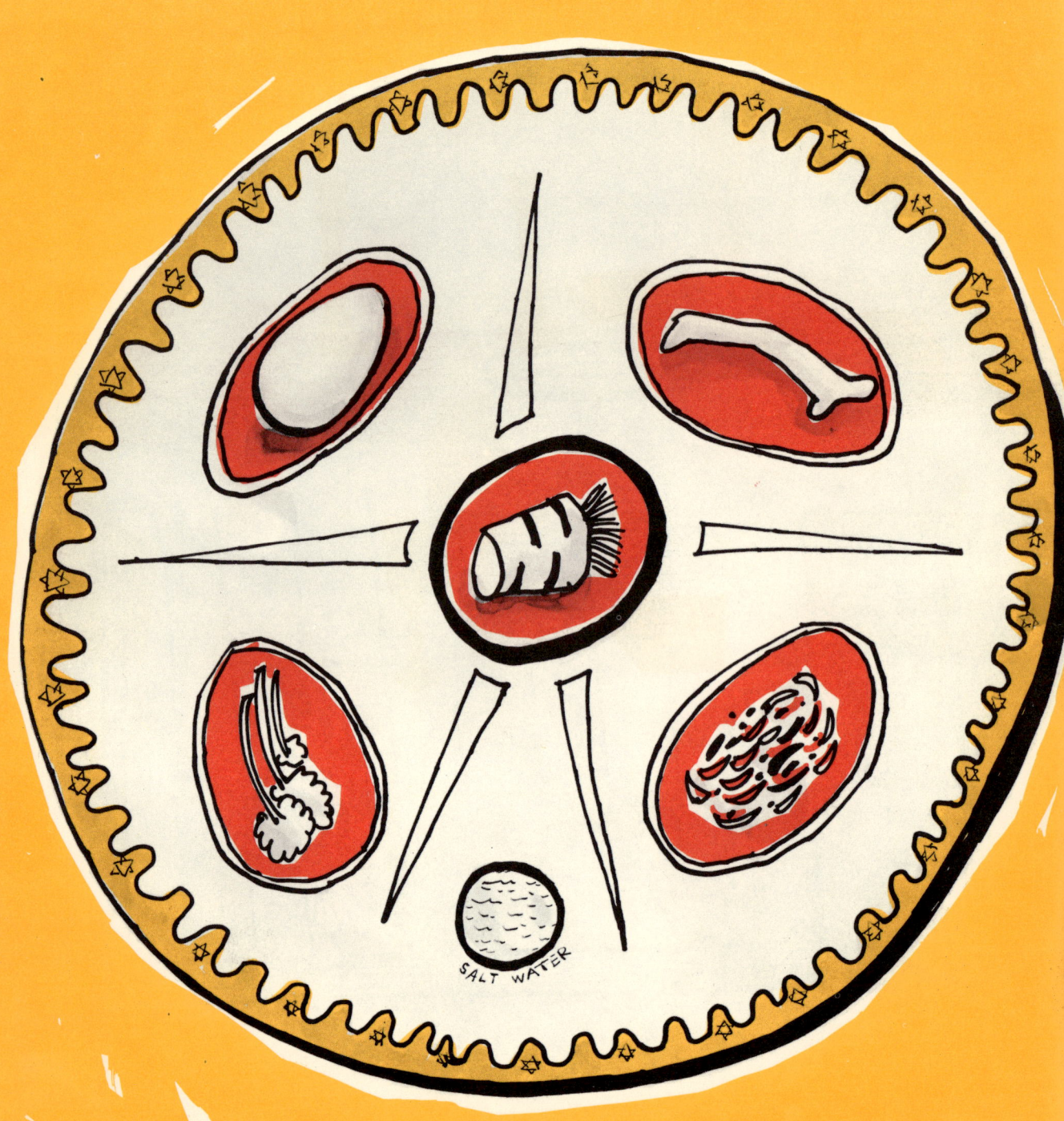

Joel became very excited. "Is the Seder going to start now?" he asked, hoping Daddy would say "yes."

"Right now, son," Daddy replied. "Grandpa has finished filling the cups with wine. So we're ready to sing the kiddush."

The kiddush melody was lovely! And how delicious the wine tasted when kiddush was over!

Joel was only half-finished with his cup when he held it out again and begged, "May I have more wine, please?" Everybody laughed.

"If you drink too much wine, now, Joel," Daddy warned, "you'll fall asleep long before the Seder is over."

Mimmy and Joel watched the grown-ups carefully as the Seder continued. Everything Grandpa, Grandma, Daddy, and Mommy did, the children wanted to do. When the grown-ups washed their hands, Mimmy and Joel washed theirs. When the grown-ups dipped the parsley greens into the salt water, so did Mimmy and Joel.

Suddenly Joel called out: "Look, Mimmy! Look what Grandpa is doing now!"

Grandpa was wrapping a piece of matzah in a big, white napkin. Then he tucked it swiftly under the tablecloth.

Mimmy grinned. She knew why Grandpa had hidden the matzah. But Joel didn't know why.

"What's Grandpa doing? Why is he hiding a piece of matzah?" he kept asking.

"Sh...sh," she whispered. "Not so loud. That's the Afikoman. We play a game with it. Grandpa hides it and whoever finds it gets a present."

"Oh, boy!" Joel exclaimed, clapping his hands with glee. "I'm going to take it. I know where it is. I saw where Grandpa put the Afi...the Afi...What did you call it, Mimmy?"

"Afikoman," she corrected him. "And besides I'm the one who's going to take it! I'm faster than you!"

"Oh no you aren't," Joel bragged.

"Wait! I have an idea, Joel," said Mimmy. "Tomorrow night we'll have another Seder. Daddy will hide the Afikoman then. You let me take Grandpa's Afikoman tonight, and I'll let you take Daddy's tomorrow night."

Joel thought about that for a while. "O.K.," he finally agreed.

Just then Daddy called out, "It's time for the *Mah Nishtanah*. Who is prepared to recite it for us?"

"I am, Daddy," said Joel, waving his hand in the air. "I know the first part."

"And I know all of it," Mimmy answered, feeling very important. "I've been practicing it for two weeks!"

"That's fine," Daddy commented. "We'll hear Joel first and then we will listen to you, Mimmy."

Joel stood up, straight as a soldier. In a loud, strong voice he sang:

"*Mah nishtanah ha-laylah ha-zeh mi-kol ha-leylot?* Why is this night so different from all other nights? *She-bekhol ha-leylot anu okhlin ḥametz umatzah, ha-laylah ha-zeh kulo matzah.* On all other nights we eat bread and rolls and baigle and crackers and matzah. But tonight we eat only matzah."

מַה נִּשְׁתַּנָּה הַלַּיְלָה הַזֶּה

"Wonderful, wonderful," Grandma and Grandpa exclaimed. "That was well done, Joel."

Now it was Mimmy's turn. Her eyes were shining happily. Proud as could be, she sang the whole *Mah Nishtanah*.

Everybody was pleased. "That was beautiful," said Mommy and Daddy, and there was a big, broad smile on their faces.

Baby Dan was sitting in his highchair near the table. He did not recite the *Mah Nishtanah*. Do you know why? Because he was too young.

Then the whole family started to read the Haggadah. Mimmy and Joel had a beautiful Haggadah with large pictures in it and bright colors. Grandpa had bought it especially for them. They turned one page after another, looking at all the beautiful pictures.

Now, what do you suppose Baby Dan was doing while everyone was reading the Haggadah? Falling asleep. It was long past his bedtime.

First he rubbed one eye with his little fingers. Then he rubbed the other. Soon his curly little head began to droop.

Mommy smiled sweetly. "My, what a sleepy little boy you are," she said. "Come, I'll tuck you into your crib." She lifted little Dan out of his highchair and carried him gently to his room.

"Well, Joel?" she asked when she returned to the table. "Are you sleepy, too?"

"Oh, no," Joel boasted. "Not me. I'm a big boy now, and I'm going to stay up for the whole Seder. You'll see!"

But did he?

Well, he didn't stay up for the *whole* Seder, but he did stay up for a *long* time. He stayed up late enough to eat the horseradish and the delicious Ḥaroset and the whole meal—the chicken and soup and matzah balls and everything.

During the meal he nibbled and nibbled at the crispy, crunchy matzot. And every once in a while, he fed Pussy, too, bending down and putting tiny pieces of chicken into the new Pesaḥ dish which he and Mimmy had bought for their kitten.

Then Grandpa said it was time to eat the Afikoman. Under the tablecloth went Grandpa's hand, reaching for the Afikoman. But it wasn't there!

"Who could have taken my Afikoman?" he wondered. Grandpa didn't have to guess very long.

Joel was so excited he let the secret out. "Mimmy took it; Mimmy took it," he shouted, jumping up and down. "She took it when you went into the kitchen to help Grandma."

"Do you really have the Afikoman?" Grandpa turned to Mimmy and asked. Mimmy was giggling so hard she couldn't talk. She just shook her head up and down.

"Well, young lady," said Grandpa, "we cannot continue the Seder without the Afikoman. That's our matzah desert. You give me the Afikoman, and I'll give you a present for it. How is that?"

"Goody, goody," Mimmy cheered. "My doll didn't get any new clothes for Pesaḥ, Grandpa. Would you buy her some."

"Certainly I'll buy some new clothes for your doll," he said. "We'll go shopping right after Yom Tov, and buy her a new dress and a new hat and new shoes."

Mimmy was so happy she ran over to Grandpa and gave him a tight hug and kiss. She also gave him the Afikoman.

Grandpa then handed everybody a small portion of it to eat.

It took Joel a long time to chew his piece. He was getting very sleepy.

Soon he began to yawn—a little yawn at first and then a bigger one. Mommy leaned over and whispered softly:

"It's very late, Joel. If you try to stay up much longer, you will be too tired to enjoy the second Seder."

Joel knew that Mommy was right. Besides, he had a special reason for wanting to be wide-awake at tomorrow's Seder. It would be his turn to take the Afikoman, and oh how he wanted a pair of shiny roller skates!

He got up from his chair and kissed everyone goodnight. Then he snapped his fingers at little Pussy.

"Here, Pussy, Pussy, Pussy," he called. "It's time for you to go to sleep, too."

"Ḥag Same'aḥ and sweet dreams, Joel," everybody said.

"Ḥag Same'aḥ and good night, everybody," he answered.

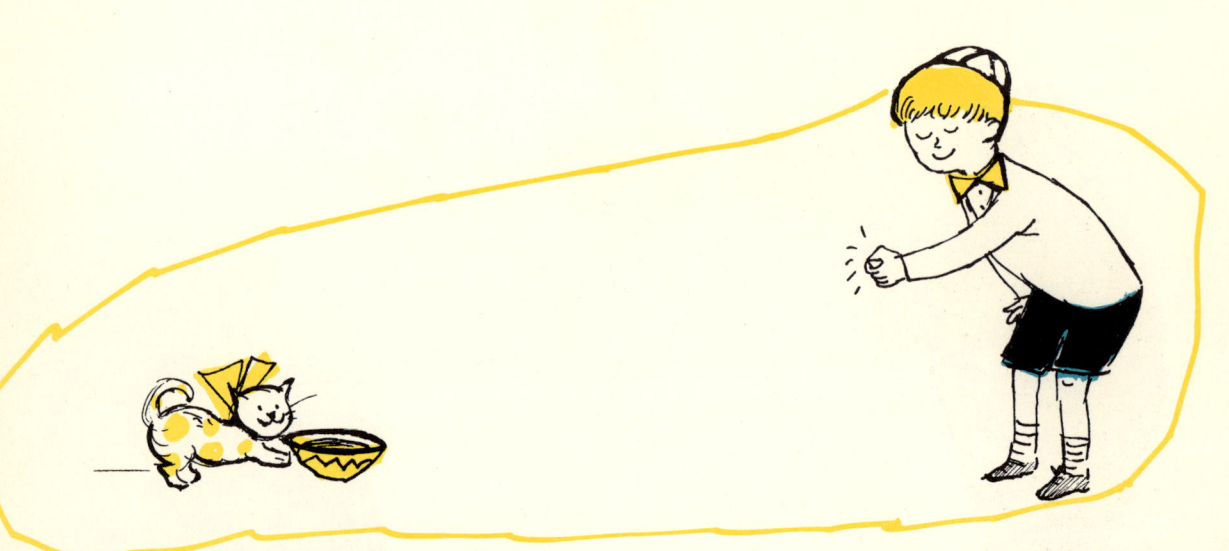

And off to bed Joel went, with Pussy scampering up the stairs behind him.

Would you like to know what happened to Mimmy?

Mimmy was a big girl. She stayed up later than Joel and sang all the lovely Seder songs she had learned in Hebrew school. This one she liked best of all:

Ḥad Gadya

Moderato

Ḥad gad - ya, ──── ḥad gad - ya,

D' - za - bin ab - ba bit - rey ── zu - zey,

Ḥad gad - ya, ──── ḥad gad - ya.

Soon Mimmy, too, became sleepy. And just as she was ready to go to bed, she turned to everybody and said:

"I love Pesaḥ. I love the songs and the matzot and the wine and the Seder and everything."

Don't you?

Glossary

Cup of Elijah — A special cup or goblet of wine set aside at the Seder for the prophet, Elijah, regarded as the emissary of the better world to come. Legend has it that Elijah visits the Seder and drinks of this cup.

Ḥad Gadya — "One Only Kid," title of the very last song in the Haggadah. It is generally regarded as an allegorical interpretation of Jewish history.

Haggadah — The book containing the special service recited at the Passover Seder.

Ḥag Same'aḥ — "Happy Holiday" in Hebrew.

Ḥaroset — A pasty compound of apples, nuts, cinnamon, and wine, symbolic of the mortar which the enslaved Israelites had to make in Egypt.

Kiddush — The ceremony, meaning "sanctification," which ushers in the Sabbath and festivals and which takes the form of a benediction pronounced over a cup of wine.

Mah Nishtanah — Opening phrase of "The Four Questions" concerning the special character of the Passover Seder, generally asked by the youngest present. The narrative of the Haggadah is in the nature of a reply.

Seder — The ceremonial meal conducted in Jewish homes on the first two evenings of the Passover holiday.

Yom Tov — Hebrew term for holiday; literally "good day."